This recipe book belongs to

....

Table of contents

Recipe	Page

Table of contents

Recipe	Page

16809392R00086

Made in the USA
Middletown, DE
25 November 2018